An Animal

KOALAS AND JOEYS

By Emilia Hendrix

 Gareth Stevens
PUBLISHING

Please visit our website, www.garethstevens.com. For a free color catalog of all our high-quality books, call toll free 1-800-542-2595 or fax 1-877-542-2596.

Library of Congress Cataloging-in-Publication Data

Hendrix, Emilia, author.
 Koalas and joeys / Emilia Hendrix.
     pages cm. — (An animal family)
 Includes index.
 ISBN 978-1-4824-3779-9 (pbk.)
 ISBN 978-1-4824-3780-5 (6 pack)
 ISBN 978-1-4824-3781-2 (library binding)
 1. Koala—Juvenile literature. 2. Koala—Behavior—Juvenile literature. I. Title.
 QL737.M384H455 2016
 599.2'5—dc23
                                    2015025058

First Edition

Published in 2016 by
Gareth Stevens Publishing
111 East 14th Street, Suite 349
New York, NY 10003

Copyright © 2016 Gareth Stevens Publishing

Editor: Ryan Nagelhout
Designer: Andrea Davison-Bartolotta

Photo credits: Cover, p. 1 Banjamint/Shutterstock.com; p. 5 Marcella Miriello/Shutterstock.com; pp. 7, 24 (fur) Sergey Berestetsky/Shutterstock.com; pp. 9, 24 (joey) Serguei Levykin/Shutterstock.com; p. 11 John Cancalosi/ Getty Images; p. 13 worldswildlifewonders/Shutterstock.com; pp. 15, 24 (pouch) Bruce Lichtenberger/ Getty Images; p. 17 James Hager/Getty Images; p. 19 Fernan Archilla/Shutterstock.com; p. 21 BMCL/ Shutterstock.com; p. 23 Pawel Papis/Shutterstock.com.

Printed in the United States of America

CPSIA compliance information: Batch #CW16GS: For further information contact Gareth Stevens, New York, New York at 1-800-542-2595.

Contents

Koalas live in trees.

They have lots of hair.
This is their fur.

Baby koalas are called joeys.

Joeys are tiny at first!

Their mothers take care of them.

Mother koalas
have pouches.

Joeys live inside them!

They stay warm
in there.

Joeys grow bigger and bigger.

21

Soon they leave
the pouch!

Words to Know

fur   joey   pouch

Index

24